SLANGMAN DAVID B

Being brought up in a multi-lingual household, David Burke used his language skills as a tour guide at Universal Studios in Hollywood, California, giving tours in English, French, Italian, and sign language. His love of language inspired him to delve into the intricacies of words and led him to become a prominent author of more than 100 books on understanding slang and idioms in different languages, as well as books that teach kids foreign languages through fairy tales. His materials on slang and idioms are currently used as course curriculum by Berlitz International, UCLA, Harvard University, NYU and Hewlett Packard, and even by the writers of The Simpsons to give Bart his coolness.

KENDALL NELSON

MA in TESOL, California State University, Los Angeles; BA in Writing, Literature, and Publishing, Emerson College. Kendall has more than six years of instructional and educational administrative experience. She has presented research at the TESOL Conference in Toronto. Kendall's research topics include trans-lingual education practices in multilingual classrooms, and storytelling methods for English language learners.

Book Design and Production: Slangman Publishing
Front Cover Illustration: Ty Semaka
Inside Illustrations: Ty Semaka

Copyright © 2019 by David Burke / Published by Slangman Publishing / Email: info@slangman.com
Website: http://www.slangman.com

ISBN: 9781947601062

Printed in the United States of America
10 9 8 7 6 5 4 3 2 1

TEACHER'S GUIDE

LESSON PREP!

- ⊙ *Optional:* Prepare the target slang words/idioms in a song or story so that students can listen to the vocabulary in context. Provide a transcript for students to read while they listen.

- ⊙ Throughout the lesson, you'll see the following icons:  and

  ⇨ *This is a great opportunity to have your students take out their mobile devices and use the QR code to access the many audio and video programs that pertain to the lesson.*

LET'S WARM UP!

MATCH THE PICTURES

1. Students discuss the topic, **AT THE PARTY**, in partners. The teacher can provide students with a handout of discussion questions.

Example questions:

☑ *What types of parties have you been to?*

☑ *What do you usually do at a party?*

☑ *What do you usually wear to parties?*

☑ *What kind of food do you like to eat at parties?*

☑ *Where was the last party you went to? What were you celebrating?*

2. The images represent the definition of the idioms/slang words both literally and figuratively. In partners, students discuss the images on pages 1 and 2 of the textbook. Have them describe what's happening in each photo.

PAGES 1-2:

⊙ Students complete the matching activity on page 2 independently.

☑ Students check their answers in partners before reviewing as a class.

LET'S TALK!

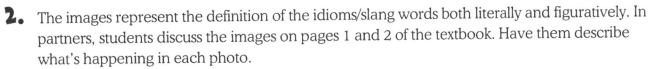

TEXT PAGES 3-4:

⊙ Students take turns practicing the dialogues as Debbie and Becky.

➡ *Challenge: For an added challenge, students can practice the dialogue in the format of READ, LOOK UP, and SAY. With this method, students read the line of dialogue silently, look up at their partner, and then say the words without looking at the book.*

LET'S USE "REAL SPEAK!"

TEXT PAGES 5-6:

⊙ Teacher presents the "Real Speak" rules to the class.

☑ Students practice the conversation on page 5 in partners using the "Real Speak" rule.

➡ *Challenge: READ, LOOK UP, and SAY. Again, students read the line of dialogue silently, look up at their partner, and then say the words without looking at the book.*

- ☉ Students complete activity **A** (**WHA'DID THEY SAY?**) independently and check their answers with a partner.

- ☉ Students complete activity **B** (**DID'JA OR DIDN'CHU?**) in groups of three. Each member of the group should practice columns 1, 2, and 3.

LET'S LEARN!

TEXT PAGES 7-10:

— Suggested Mini-Lessons —

- ☉ Provide small groups of 3-4 students with matching cards of idioms/slang and their definitions. Students mix up the cards and place them face down on the desk. Students take turns flipping over cards looking for matches. The student who has the most matches at the end wins!

- ☉ In the groups of 3-4, each student is assigned an equal portion of the 12 idioms on pages 7-10. Each student reads his/her section of assigned idioms and creates a sentence for the **"Now you do it"** section of the idioms. After completing, each student shares his/her sample sentence with the rest of the group.

- ☉ In pairs, students complete the **"Now you do it"** sections orally for each idiom. Each student in the pair must come up with a new sentence for each idiom.

LET'S PRACTICE!

TEXT PAGES 11-12:

— Suggested Mini-Lesson —

- ☉ Students complete the practice activities on these pages independently first and then check their answers in pairs. After the pair check is complete, the answers are reviewed as a class.

  - ⮕ *Challenge: Have a strong student lead the class review of answers, calling on students and asking them to provide rationale for their answers.*

⊙ Students work in partners to practice conversations 1-10. The pair should take turns asking and answering questions.

➡ *Challenge: Before having students look at page 13, provide them with a copy in which the "Person B" column has the answers jumbled. Have students try to match the questions to the answers before completing the activity.*

➡ *Challenge: After they practice the conversations, have students continue the conversations (1-10) in front of the class. They can write out a script or simply role play on the spot.*

WORKBOOK EXERCISES + EXPANSION

TEXT PAGES 14-19

⊙ Students can engage in the following expansion activities for both **THE SLANGMAN FILES** as well as the target idioms/slang presented in the unit:

1. **Written Production:** Have students create a dialogue or story with the target idioms/slang and perform it or read it in front of the class. Make it a contest! See which group can use the most idioms correctly in their dialogue/story.

2. **Spoken Production:** Have students engage in a timed role play in pairs in front of the class. Provide them each with a different set of target idioms/slang that they need to use during the role play.

3. **Visual Activity:** Have students play Pictionary® in groups. Each student chooses a target idiom/slang word from the unit and draws an image that captures the meaning. Group members will try to guess the correct idiom/slang word. The student who guesses the most idioms correctly in the group is the winner.

➡ *Challenge: Students cannot use the textbook when they are guessing the idioms/slang words.*

POST-UNIT ACTIVITY:

⊙ As a class, tune in to **SLANGMAN FRIDAYS** which features a new episode on idioms and slang used on TV each week - **https://www.youtube.com/SlangmanTV** and *MAKE SURE THAT EACH STUDENT SUBSCRIBES!*

☑ The video can be used as a final component of the unit and used as a warm-up/review before the next unit begins. Optional activities for the warm-up/review include:

1. Fill in the blank activity with target slang/idioms used in the video.

2. Sentence creation with target idioms/slang.

3. Dialogue/story creation with target idioms/slang.

4. *Teaching by students:* Assign each student or pair one of the idioms/slang words explained in the video and ask them to teach it to the rest of the class with at least one context example.

TEACHER NOTES

TEACHER'S GUIDE

LESSON PREP!

- ⊙ *Optional:* Prepare the target slang words/idioms in a song or story so that students can listen to the vocabulary in context. Provide a transcript for students to read while they listen.

- ⊙ Throughout the lesson, you'll see the following icons:  and

  ➡ *This is a great opportunity to have your students take out their mobile devices and use the QR code to access the many audio and video programs that pertain to the lesson.*

LET'S WARM UP!

MATCH THE PICTURES

1. Students discuss the topic, **AT THE MARKET**, in partners. The teacher can provide students with a handout of discussion questions.

<u>Example questions:</u>

☑ What do you usually buy at the market?

☑ What is your favorite market?

☑ What do you spend the most money on at the market?

☑ What is the healthiest thing you buy at the market?

☑ What's your guilty pleasure (the least healthy thing you buy at the market)?

2. The images represent the definition of the idioms/slang words both literally and figuratively. In partners, students discuss the images on pages 21 and 22 of the textbook. Have them describe what's happening in each photo.

PAGES 21-22:

⊙ Students complete the matching activity on page 22 independently.

☑ Students check their answers in partners before reviewing as a class.

LET'S TALK!

TEXT PAGES 23-24:

⊙ Students take turns practicing the dialogues as Bill and Liz.

➦ *Challenge: For an added challenge, students can practice the dialogue in the format of READ, LOOK UP, and SAY. With this method, students read the line of dialogue silently, look up at their partner, and then say the words without looking at the book.*

LET'S USE "REAL SPEAK!"

TEXT PAGES 25-26:

⊙ Teacher presents the "Real Speak" rules to the class.

☑ Students practice the conversation on page 25 in partners using the "Real Speak" rule.

➦ *Challenge: READ, LOOK UP, and SAY. Again, students read the line of dialogue silently, look up at their partner, and then say the words without looking at the book.*

⊙ Students complete activity **A** (**"T" PRONOUNCED LIKE "D"**) on page 26 independently and check their answers with a partner.

☑ Students take turns saying the statements in activity **A** practicing the "d" sound.

LET'S LEARN!

TEXT PAGES 27-29:

— Suggested Mini-Lessons —

⊙ Provide pairs of students with a set of copies of pages 27-29 with the target idioms and slang replaced with blank lines. Students work together to fill in the blanks with the target idiom/slang word.

☑ Students check their answers in the book.

⊙ In pairs, each student is assigned an equal portion of the 10 idioms on pages 27-29. Each student reads his/her section of assigned idioms and creates a sentence for the **"Now you do it"** section of the idioms. After completing, each student shares his/her sample sentence with the rest of the group.

⊙ In pairs, students complete the **"Now you do it"** sections orally for each idiom. Each student in the pair must come up with a new sentence for each idiom.

LET'S PRACTICE!

TEXT PAGE 30:

— Suggested Mini-Lessons —

⊙ Students listen to the commercial while they read along silently. Then, have students take turns reading it aloud in partners.

☑ Students write answers to questions in partners.

⊙ Students take turns practicing the questions and answers for numbers 1-6 verbally.

➥ *Challenge: Have students get in small groups to plan and perform the commercial in front of the class. Encourage them to add on and get creative with the content!*

TEXT PAGE 31-32:

⦿ Students complete the practice activities on these pages independently first and then check their answers in pairs. After the pair check is complete, the answers are reviewed as a class.

➲ *Challenge: Have a strong student lead the class review of answers, calling on students and asking them to provide rationale for their answers.*

WORKBOOK EXERCISES + EXPANSION

TEXT PAGES 33-39:

⦿ Students can engage in the following expansion activities for both **THE SLANGMAN FILES** as well as the target idioms/slang presented in the unit:

1. **Written Production:** Have students create a dialogue or story with the target idioms/slang and perform it or read it in front of the class. Make it a contest! See which group can use the most idioms correctly in their dialogue/story.

2. **Spoken Production:** Have students engage in a timed role play in pairs in front of the class. Provide them each with a different set of target idioms/slang that they need to use during the role play.

3. **Visual Activity:** Have students play Pictionary® in groups. Each student chooses a target idiom/slang word from the unit and draws an image that captures the meaning. Group members will try to guess the correct idiom/slang word. The student who guesses the most idioms correctly in the group is the winner.

➲ *Challenge: Students cannot use the textbook when they are guessing the idioms/slang words.*

POST-UNIT ACTIVITY:

⊙ As a class, tune in to **SLANGMAN FRIDAYS** which features a new episode on idioms and slang used on TV each week - **https://www.youtube.com/SlangmanTV** and *MAKE SURE THAT EACH STUDENT SUBSCRIBES!*

☑ The video can be used as a final component of the unit and used as a warm-up/review before the next unit begins. Optional activities for the warm-up/review include:

1. Fill in the blank activity with target slang/idioms used in the video.

2. Sentence creation with target idioms/slang.

3. Dialog/story creation with target idioms/slang.

4. *Teaching by students:* Assign each student or pair one of the idioms/slang words explained in the video and ask them to teach it to the rest of the class with at least one context example.

TEACHER NOTES

TEACHER'S GUIDE

LESSON PREP!

- ⊙ *Optional:* Prepare the target slang words/idioms in a song or story so that students can listen to the vocabulary in context. Provide a transcript for students to read while they listen.

- ⊙ Throughout the lesson, you'll see the following icons:  and

  ⤳ *This is a great opportunity to have your students take out their mobile devices and use the QR code to access the many audio and video programs that pertain to the lesson.*

LET'S WARM UP!

MATCH THE PICTURES

1. Students discuss the topic, **AT THE MOVIES**, in partners. The teacher can provide students with a handout of discussion questions.

Example questions:

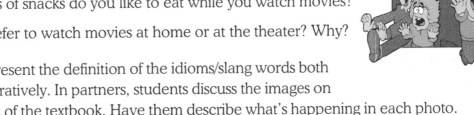

- ☑ What are your favorite types of movies?

- ☑ When was the last time you went to the movie theater?

- ☑ What did you see the last time you went to the theater?

- ☑ What kinds of snacks do you like to eat while you watch movies?

- ☑ Do you prefer to watch movies at home or at the theater? Why?

2. The images represent the definition of the idioms/slang words both literally and figuratively. In partners, students discuss the images on pages 41 and 42 of the textbook. Have them describe what's happening in each photo.

PAGES 41-42:

- ⊙ Students complete the matching activity on page 42 independently.

  - ☑ Students check their answers in partners before reviewing as a class.

LET'S TALK!

TEXT PAGES 43-44:

- ⊙ Students take turns practicing the dialogues as George and David.

  - ➥ *Challenge: For an added challenge, students can practice the dialogue in the format of READ, LOOK UP, and SAY. With this method, students read the line of dialogue silently, look up at their partner, and then say the words without looking at the book.*

LET'S USE "REAL SPEAK!"

TEXT PAGES 45-46:

- ⊙ Teacher presents the "Real Speak" rules to the class.

  - ☑ Students practice the conversation on page 45 in partners using the "Real Speak" rule.

    - ➥ *Challenge: READ, LOOK UP, and SAY. Again, students read the line of dialogue silently, look up at their partner, and then say the words without looking at the book.*

⊙ Students complete activity **A** (**SHOULD'A, COULD'A, WOULD'A, MUST'A**) on page 46 independently and check their answers with a partner.

☑ Students take turns saying the statements in activity **A** practicing the target "Real Speak" sound.

LET'S LEARN!

TEXT PAGES 47-50:

— *Suggested Mini-Lessons* —

⊙ Provide each student with either the target idiom/slang words OR the translations. For instance, if a student has three idioms/slang words, another student has the matching three translations. Then, have students physically find the student who has their matches.

☑ Once students find each other, they work with the idioms/slang words that they just matched from pages 47-50.

☑ Each pair reads their section of assigned idioms and creates a sentence for the **"Now you do it"** section of the idioms. After completing, each pair shares their sample sentence with another pair.

⊙ In pairs, students complete the **"Now you do it"** sections orally for each idiom. Each student in the pair must come up with a new sentence for each idiom.

LET'S PRACTICE!

TEXT PAGE 51-52:

⊙ Students complete the practice activities on these pages independently first and then check their answers in pairs. After the pair check is complete, the answers are reviewed as a class.

➲ *Challenge: Have a strong student lead the class review of answers, calling on students and asking them to provide rationale for their answers.*

TEXT PAGES 53

— *Suggested Activity* —

⊙ Have students get into pairs. Give each pair one of the scenarios on page 53 as well as one set of idioms/slang words from the box.

➡ *Option 1: Have students do an on-the-spot role play in front of the class using the scenario and target vocabulary.*

➡ *Option 2: Have students write a dialog using the scenario and target vocabulary and perform it in front of the class.*

WORKBOOK EXERCISES + EXPANSION

TEXT PAGES 33-39

⊙ Students can engage in the following expansion activities for both **THE SLANGMAN FILES** as well as the target idioms/slang presented in the unit:

1. **Written Production:** Have students create a dialogue or story with the target idioms/slang and perform it or read it in front of the class. Make it a contest! See which group can use the most idioms correctly in their dialogue/story.

2. **Spoken Production:** Have students engage in a timed role play in pairs in front of the class. Provide them each with a different set of target idioms/slang that they need to use during the role play.

3. **Visual Activity:** Have students play Pictionary® in groups. Each student chooses a target idiom/slang word from the unit and draws an image that captures the meaning. Group members will try to guess the correct idiom/slang word. The student who guesses the most idioms correctly in the group is the winner.

➡ *Challenge: Students cannot use the textbook when they are guessing the idioms/slang words.*

POST-UNIT ACTIVITY:

⊙ As a class, tune in to **SLANGMAN FRIDAYS** which features a new episode on idioms and slang used on TV each week - **https://www.youtube.com/SlangmanTV** and *MAKE SURE THAT EACH STUDENT SUBSCRIBES!*

☑ The video can be used as a final component of the unit and used as a warm-up/review before the next unit begins. Optional activities for the warm-up/review include:

1. Fill in the blank activity with target slang/idioms used in the video.

2. Sentence creation with target idioms/slang.

3. Dialog/story creation with target idioms/slang.

4. *Teaching by students:* Assign each student or pair one of the idioms/slang words explained in the video and ask them to teach it to the rest of the class with at least one context example.

TEACHER NOTES

TEACHER'S GUIDE

LESSON PREP!

⊙ *Optional:* Prepare the target slang words/idioms in a song or story so that students can listen to the vocabulary in context. Provide a transcript for students to read while they listen.

⊙ Throughout the lesson, you'll see the following icons:  and

↪ *This is a great opportunity to have your students take out their mobile devices and use the QR code to access the many audio and video programs that pertain to the lesson.*

LET'S WARM UP!

MATCH THE PICTURES

1. Students discuss the topic, **ON VACATION**, in partners. The teacher can provide students with a handout of discussion questions.

Example questions:

☑ Where have you gone on vacation?

☑ What is your favorite trip you've ever taken?

☑ What kinds of things do you like to do on vacation?

☑ Where would you like to go on vacation that you haven't been before?

☑ Who do you like to travel with? Why?

2. The images represent the definition of the idioms/slang words both literally and figuratively. In partners, students discuss the images on pages 61 and 62 of the textbook. Have them describe what's happening in each photo.

PAGES 61-62:

⊙ Students complete the matching activity on page 62 independently.

☑ Students check their answers in partners before reviewing as a class.

LET'S TALK!

TEXT PAGES 63-64:

⊙ Students take turns practicing the dialogues as Chris and Marie.

➥ *Challenge: For an added challenge, students can practice the dialogue in the format of READ, LOOK UP, and SAY. With this method, students read the line of dialogue silently, look up at their partner, and then say the words without looking at the book.*

LET'S USE "REAL SPEAK!"

TEXT PAGES 65-66:

⊙ Teacher presents the "Real Speak" rules to the class.

☑ Students practice the conversation on page 65 in partners using the "Real Speak" rule.

⮑ *Challenge: READ, LOOK UP, and SAY. Again, students read the line of dialogue silently, look up at their partner, and then say the words without looking at the book.*

◉ Students complete activity **A (PUT THE PAIRS BACK TOGETHER)** on page 66 independently and check their answers with a partner.

☑ Students take turns saying the statements in activity **A** practicing the target "Real Speak" sound.

⮑ *Challenge: Provide pairs with only one half of the common word pairs and have students try to produce the other half before checking on page 66.*

LET'S LEARN!

TEXT PAGES 67–69:

— *Suggested Mini-Lessons* —

◉ Provide each student with an idiom/slang word from pages 67-69. Have each student draw a picture that represents his/her word or phrase.

☑ Have students get in small groups and try to guess the slang word/idiom associated with the pictures.

◉ Assign each student a section of idioms/slang words from pages 67-69.

☑ Each student reads his/her section of assigned idioms and creates a sentence for the **"Now you do it"** section of the idioms. After completing, each student shares his/her sample sentence with the rest of the group.

◉ In pairs, students complete the **"Now you do it"** sections orally for each idiom. Each student in the pair must come up with a new sentence for each idiom.

LET'S PRACTICE!

TEXT PAGE 70–72:

◉ Students complete the practice activities on these pages independently first and then check their answers in pairs. After the pair check is complete, the answers are reviewed as a class.

➡ *Challenge: For the activity on pages 71 and 72, create a game wheels with a spinner that includes the target vocabulary from one of the two pages. Students work in small groups taking turns spinning the spinner. When the spinner lands on a slang word/idiom or its translation, students should provide its match. Students can make it a friendly competition by keeping track of how many answers they get correct.*

WORKBOOK EXERCISES + EXPANSION

TEXT PAGES 73-85:

◉ Students can engage in the following expansion activities for both **THE SLANGMAN FILES** as well as the target idioms/slang presented in the unit:

1. **Written Production:** Have students create a dialogue or story with the target idioms/slang and perform it or read it in front of the class. Make it a contest! See which group can use the most idioms correctly in their dialogue/story.

2. **Spoken Production:** Have students engage in a timed role play in pairs in front of the class. Provide them each with a different set of target idioms/slang that they need to use during the role play.

3. **Visual Activity:** Have students play Pictionary® in groups. Each student chooses a target idiom/slang word from the unit and draws an image that captures the meaning. Group members will try to guess the correct idiom/slang word. The student who guesses the most idioms correctly in the group is the winner.

➡ *Challenge: Students cannot use the textbook when they are guessing the idioms/slang words.*

POST-UNIT ACTIVITY:

⊙ As a class, tune in to **SLANGMAN FRIDAYS** which features a new episode on idioms and slang used on TV each week - **https://www.youtube.com/SlangmanTV** and *MAKE SURE THAT EACH STUDENT SUBSCRIBES!*

☑ The video can be used as a final component of the unit and used as a warm-up/review before the next unit begins. Optional activities for the warm-up/review include:

1. Fill in the blank activity with target slang/idioms used in the video.

2. Sentence creation with target idioms/slang.

3. Dialog/story creation with target idioms/slang.

4. *Teaching by students:* Assign each student or pair one of the idioms/slang words explained in the video and ask them to teach it to the rest of the class with at least one context example.

TEACHER NOTES

TEACHER'S GUIDE

LESSON PREP!

- ⊙ *Optional:* Prepare the target slang words/idioms in a song or story so that students can listen to the vocabulary in context. Provide a transcript for students to read while they listen.

- ⊙ Throughout the lesson, you'll see the following icons:  and

  ⇨ *This is a great opportunity to have your students take out their mobile devices and use the QR code to access the many audio and video programs that pertain to the lesson.*

LET'S WARM UP!

MATCH THE PICTURES

1. Students discuss the topic, **AT THE AIRPORT**, in partners. The teacher can provide students with a handout of discussion questions.

Example questions:

☑ How do you feel when you have to go to the airport?

☑ Do you like going on airplanes? Why or why not?

☑ What do you normally bring with you to the airport?

☑ What is your favorite part about the airport?

☑ What is your least favorite part about the airport?

2. The images represent the definition of the idioms/slang words both literally and figuratively. In partners, students discuss the images on pages 87 and 88 of the textbook. Have them describe what's happening in each photo.

PAGES 87-88:

⊙ Students complete the matching activity on page 88 independently.

☑ Students check their answers in partners before reviewing as a class.

LET'S TALK!

TEXT PAGES 89-90:

⊙ Students take turns practicing the dialogues as Steve and Karen.

➡ *Challenge: For an added challenge, students can practice the dialogue in the format of READ, LOOK UP, and SAY. With this method, students read the line of dialogue silently, look up at their partner, and then say the words without looking at the book.*

LET'S USE "REAL SPEAK!"

TEXT PAGES 91-92:

⊙ Teacher presents the "Real Speak" rules to the class.

☑ Students practice the conversation on page 91 in partners using the "Real Speak" rule.

➡ *Challenge: READ, LOOK UP, and SAY. Again, students read the line of dialogue silently, look up at their partner, and then say the words without looking at the book.*

⊙ Students complete activity **B ("TA BE" OR NOT "TA BE...")** on page 92 independently and check their answers with a partner.

☑ Students take turns saying the statements in activity **B** practicing the target "Real Speak" sound.

⮕ *Challenge: Have students write original sentences using the target "Real Speak" and practice them in partners.*

LET'S LEARN!

TEXT PAGES 93-95:

— *Suggested Mini-Lessons* —

⊙ Provide students with the translations of the idioms/slang words in a word bank.

☑ Have students listen to the "Real Speak" versions of the idioms/slang words without looking in their textbooks.

☑ Have students write down the translation for each "Real Speak" version of the idiom/slang word.

⊙ Assign each student a section of idioms/slang words from pages 93-95.

☑ Each student reads his/her section of assigned idioms and creates a sentence for the **"Now you do it"** section of the idioms. After completing, each student shares his/her sample sentence with the rest of the group.

⊙ In pairs, students complete the **"Now you do it"** sections orally for each idiom. Each student in the pair must come up with a new sentence for each idiom.

LET'S PRACTICE!

TEXT PAGE 96-98:

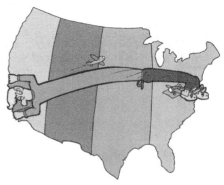

⊙ Students complete the practice activities on these pages independently first and then check their answers in pairs. After the pair check is complete, the answers are reviewed as a class.

➲ *Challenge: To expand on the fairytale exercise on page 96, have students work in pairs to create their own fairytale stories. Provide each pair with a set of target idioms/slang words that they must incorporate into their fairytale. When they're finished, the pair will read their fairytale in front of the class.*

WORKBOOK EXERCISES + EXPANSION

TEXT PAGES 99–107

◉ Students can engage in the following expansion activities for both **THE SLANGMAN FILES** as well as the target idioms/slang presented in the unit:

1. **Written Production:** Have students create a dialogue or story with the target idioms/slang and perform it or read it in front of the class. Make it a contest! See which group can use the most idioms correctly in their dialogue/story.

2. **Spoken Production:** Have students engage in a timed role play in pairs in front of the class. Provide them each with a different set of target idioms/slang that they need to use during the role play.

3. **Visual Activity:** Have students play Pictionary® in groups. Each student chooses a target idiom/slang word from the unit and draws an image that captures the meaning. Group members will try to guess the correct idiom/slang word. The student who guesses the most idioms correctly in the group is the winner.

➲ *Challenge: Students cannot use the textbook when they are guessing the idioms/slang words.*

POST-UNIT ACTIVITY:

⊙ As a class, tune in to **SLANGMAN FRIDAYS** which features a new episode on idioms and slang used on TV each week - **https://www.youtube.com/SlangmanTV** and *MAKE SURE THAT EACH STUDENT SUBSCRIBES!*

☑ The video can be used as a final component of the unit and used as a warm-up/review before the next unit begins. Optional activities for the warm-up/review include:

1. Fill in the blank activity with target slang/idioms used in the video.

2. Sentence creation with target idioms/slang.

3. Dialog/story creation with target idioms/slang.

4. *Teaching by students:* Assign each student or pair one of the idioms/slang words explained in the video and ask them to teach it to the rest of the class with at least one context example.

TEACHER NOTES

TEACHER'S GUIDE

LESSON PREP!

- ⊙ *Optional*: Prepare the target slang words/idioms in a song or story so that students can listen to the vocabulary in context. Provide a transcript for students to read while they listen.

- ⊙ Throughout the lesson, you'll see the following icons:  and

  ➲ *This is a great opportunity to have your students take out their mobile devices and use the QR code to access the many audio and video programs that pertain to the lesson.*

LET'S WARM UP!

MATCH THE PICTURES

1. Students discuss the topic, **AT A RESTAURANT**, in partners. The teacher can provide students with a handout of discussion questions.

Example questions:

☑ What is your favorite restaurant? Why is it your favorite?

☑ What is your favorite kind of food?

☑ How often do you eat at restaurants?

☑ What is the worst restaurant you have ever been to? Why was it the worst?

☑ What is your least favorite type of food?

2. The images represent the definition of the idioms/slang words both literally and figuratively. In partners, students discuss the images on pages 109 and 110 of the textbook. Have them describe what's happening in each photo.

PAGES 109-110:

⊙ Students complete the matching activity on page 110 independently.

☑ Students check their answers in partners before reviewing as a class.

LET'S TALK!

TEXT PAGES 111-112:

⊙ Students take turns practicing the dialogues as Cecily and Jim.

↪ *Challenge: For an added challenge, students can practice the dialogue in the format of READ, LOOK UP, and SAY. With this method, students read the line of dialogue silently, look up at their partner, and then say the words without looking at the book.*

LET'S USE "REAL SPEAK!"

TEXT PAGES 113-114:

⊙ Teacher presents the "Real Speak" rules to the class.

☑ Students practice the conversation on page 113 in partners using the "Real Speak" rule.

➲ *Challenge: READ, LOOK UP, and SAY. Again, students read the line of dialogue silently, look up at their partner, and then say the words without looking at the book.*

⊙ In partners, students take turns practicing the sentences in activity **A (NOW YOU'RE GONNA DO A "GONNA" EXERCISE)** on page 114.

⊙ For activity **B (IS IT "GONNA" OR "GOING TO"?)** on page 114, one student reads the paragraph to his/her partner. The other student, after numbering a piece of paper 1-8, writes down either "**gonna**" or "**going to**" accordingly. Then, the student writing checks the answers by reading the passage aloud.

➲ *Challenge: Have students write original sentences using the target "Real Speak" and practice them in partners.*

— *Suggested Mini-Lessons* —

⊙ Provide small groups of 3-4 students with matching cards of idioms/slang from pages 115-118 and their definitions. Students mix up the cards and place them face down on the desk. Students take turns flipping over cards looking for matches. The student who has the most matches at the end wins!

⊙ Assign each student a section of idioms/slang words from pages 115-118.

☑ Each student reads his/her section of assigned idioms and creates a sentence for the **"Now you do it"** section of the idioms. After completing, each student shares his/her sample sentence with the rest of the group.

⊙ In pairs, students complete the **"Now you do it"** sections orally for each idiom. Each student in the pair must come up with a new sentence for each idiom.

LET'S PRACTICE!

TEXT PAGE 118-121:

⊙ Students complete the practice activities on these pages independently first and then check their answers in pairs. After the pair check is complete, the answers are reviewed as a class.

⟶ *Challenge: To expand on the matching exercise on page 121, have students get into pairs or small groups to do a restaurant role play in front of the class. Provide them a written scenario of the roleplay. They should try and use as many target idioms/slang words as possible. The team that uses the most is the winner!*

TEXT PAGE 122:

⊙ Students complete the matching activity independently before checking their answers with a partner. Answers are reviewed as a class.

⟶ *Expansion: Create a digital game (like Jeopardy! or Kahoot!) with sentences that are missing the target idiom/slang word. Students are put in partners and compete with other partners to get the most answers correct.*

WORKBOOK EXERCISES + EXPANSION

TEXT PAGES 123-127:

⊙ Students can engage in the following expansion activities for both **THE SLANGMAN FILES** as well as the target idioms/slang presented in the unit:

1. **Written Production:** Have students create a dialogue or story with the target idioms/slang and perform it or read it in front of the class. Make it a contest! See which group can use the most idioms correctly in their dialogue/story.

2. **Spoken Production:** Have students engage in a timed role play in pairs in front of the class. Provide them each with a different set of target idioms/slang that they need to use during the role play.

3. **Visual Activity:** Have students play Pictionary® in groups. Each student chooses a target idiom/slang word from the unit and draws an image that captures the meaning. Group members will try to guess the correct idiom/slang word. The student who guesses the most idioms correctly in the group is the winner.

➡ *Challenge: Students cannot use the textbook when they are guessing the idioms/slang words.*

POST-UNIT ACTIVITY:

⦿ As a class, tune in to **SLANGMAN FRIDAYS** which features a new episode on idioms and slang used on TV each week - **https://www.youtube.com/SlangmanTV** and *MAKE SURE THAT EACH STUDENT SUBSCRIBES!*

☑ The video can be used as a final component of the unit and used as a warm-up/review before the next unit begins. Optional activities for the warm-up/review include:

1. Fill in the blank activity with target slang/idioms used in the video.

2. Sentence creation with target idioms/slang.

3. Dialog/story creation with target idioms/slang.

4. *Teaching by students:* Assign each student or pair one of the idioms/slang words explained in the video and ask them to teach it to the rest of the class with at least one context example.

TEACHER NOTES

TEACHER'S GUIDE

LESSON PREP!

- ⊙ *Optional:* Prepare the target slang words/idioms in a song or story so that students can listen to the vocabulary in context. Provide a transcript for students to read while they listen.

- ⊙ Throughout the lesson, you'll see the following icons:  and

  ⟹ *This is a great opportunity to have your students take out their mobile devices and use the QR code to access the many audio and video programs that pertain to the lesson.*

LET'S WARM UP!

MATCH THE PICTURES

1. Students discuss the topic, **ON THE ROAD**, in partners. The teacher can provide students with a handout of discussion questions.

<u>Example questions:</u>

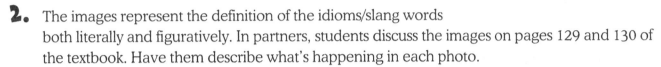

☑ Have you ever taken a road trip (or driven somewhere for vacation)?

☑ Where have you gone on a road trip?

☑ Do you like riding in the car? Why or why not?

☑ What are the best snacks to bring on a road trip?

☑ Where is the farthest you have ever driven?

2. The images represent the definition of the idioms/slang words both literally and figuratively. In partners, students discuss the images on pages 129 and 130 of the textbook. Have them describe what's happening in each photo.

PAGES 129-130:

⊙ Students complete the matching activity on page 130 independently.

  ☑ Students check their answers in partners before reviewing as a class.

LET'S TALK!

TEXT PAGES 131-132:

⊙ Students take turns practicing the dialogues as Mark and John.

  ➡ *Challenge: For an added challenge, students can practice the dialogue in the format of READ, LOOK UP, and SAY. With this method, students read the line of dialogue silently, look up at their partner, and then say the words without looking at the book.*

LET'S USE "REAL SPEAK!"

TEXT PAGES 133-134:

⊙ Teacher presents the "Real Speak" rules to the class.

☑ Students practice the conversation on page 133 in partners using the "Real Speak" rule.

⟹ *Challenge: READ, LOOK UP, and SAY. Again, students read the line of dialogue silently, look up at their partner, and then say the words without looking at the book.*

⊙ In partners, students take turns practicing column A and B in activity **A (WANNA OR WANSTA)** on page 134.

⟹ *Challenge: Have students write original sentences using the target "Real Speak" and practice them in partners.*

LET'S LEARN!

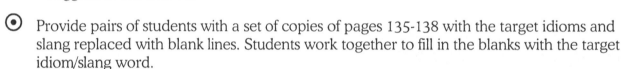

TEXT PAGES 135–138:

— *Suggested Mini-Lessons* —

⊙ Provide pairs of students with a set of copies of pages 135-138 with the target idioms and slang replaced with blank lines. Students work together to fill in the blanks with the target idiom/slang word.

☑ Students check their answers in the book.

⊙ In pairs, each student is assigned an equal portion of the 14 idioms on pages 135-138. Each student reads his/her section of assigned idioms and creates a sentence for the "**Now you do it**" section of the idioms. After completing, each student shared his/her sample sentence with the rest of the group.

⊙ In pairs, students complete the **"Now you do it"** sections orally for each idiom. Each student in the pair must come up with a new sentence for each idiom.

LET'S PRACTICE!

TEXT PAGE 139–142:

⊙ Students complete the practice activities on these pages independently first and then check their answers in pairs. After the pair check is complete, the answers are reviewed as a class.

➲ *Challenge: Have students get in partners and pretend they are the teachers. They create their own practice activity with the target idioms/slang words. Then, they give their activity to another group to complete.*

WORKBOOK EXERCISES + EXPANSION

TEXT PAGES 143-149:

◉ Students can engage in the following expansion activities for both **THE SLANGMAN FILES** as well as the target idioms/slang presented in the unit:

1. **Written Production:** Have students create a dialogue or story with the target idioms/slang and perform it or read it in front of the class. Make it a contest! See which group can use the most idioms correctly in their dialogue/story.

2. **Spoken Production:** Have students engage in a timed role play in pairs in front of the class. Provide them each with a different set of target idioms/slang that they need to use during the role play.

3. **Visual Activity:** Have students play Pictionary® in groups. Each student chooses a target idiom/slang word from the unit and draws an image that captures the meaning. Group members will try to guess the correct idiom/slang word. The student who guesses the most idioms correctly in the group is the winner.

➲ *Challenge: Students cannot use the textbook when they are guessing the idioms/slang words.*

POST-UNIT ACTIVITY:

⊙ As a class, tune in to **SLANGMAN FRIDAYS** which features a new episode on idioms and slang used on TV each week - **https://www.youtube.com/SlangmanTV** and *MAKE SURE THAT EACH STUDENT SUBSCRIBES!*

☑ The video can be used as a final component of the unit and used as a warm-up/review before the next unit begins. Optional activities for the warm-up/review include:

1. Fill in the blank activity with target slang/idioms used in the video.

2. Sentence creation with target idioms/slang.

3. Dialog/story creation with target idioms/slang.

4. *Teaching by students:* Assign each student or pair one of the idioms/slang words explained in the video and ask them to teach it to the rest of the class with at least one context example.

TEACHER NOTES

TEACHER'S GUIDE

LESSON PREP!

- ⊙ *Optional:* Prepare the target slang words/idioms in a song or story so that students can listen to the vocabulary in context. Provide a transcript for students to read while they listen.

- ⊙ Throughout the lesson, you'll see the following icons:  and

  ⮩ *This is a great opportunity to have your students take out their mobile devices and use the QR code to access the many audio and video programs that pertain to the lesson.*

LET'S WARM UP!

MATCH THE PICTURES

1. Students discuss the topic, **AT SCHOOL**, in partners. The teacher can provide students with a handout of discussion questions.

Example questions:

- ☑ What was your favorite subject in school?
- ☑ What was your least favorite subject?
- ☑ Who was your favorite teacher in school? Why?
- ☑ If you could be a teacher, what would you teach?
- ☑ Are you good at taking tests? Why or why not?

2. The images represent the definition of the idioms/slang words both literally and figuratively. In partners, students discuss the images on pages 151 and 152 of the textbook. Have them describe what's happening in each photo.

PAGES 151-152:

- ⊙ Students complete the matching activity on page 152 independently.

  - ☑ Students check their answers in partners before reviewing as a class.

LET'S TALK!

TEXT PAGES 153-154:

- ⊙ Students take turns practicing the dialogues as David and Nancy.

  - ➡ *Challenge: For an added challenge, students can practice the dialogue in the format of READ, LOOK UP, and SAY. With this method, students read the line of dialogue silently, look up at their partner, and then say the words without looking at the book.*

LET'S USE "REAL SPEAK!"

TEXT PAGES 155-156:

- ⊙ Teacher presents the "Real Speak" rules to the class.

  - ☑ Students practice the conversation on page 155 in partners using the "Real Speak" rule.

⮑ *Challenge: READ, LOOK UP, and SAY. Again, students read the line of dialogue silently, look up at their partner, and then say the words without looking at the book.*

◉ In partners, students complete activity **A (CHANGE 'EM TO REAL SPEAK)** on page 156 independently first and then check their answers in partners.

⮑ *Challenge: Have each student write a short story similar to the one in activity A on page 156. Require them to use the target "Real Speak" as well as words that look the same but DON'T use the "Real Speak" rule. Have students switch their stories with a partner to practice reading aloud.*

LET'S LEARN!

TEXT PAGES 157-160:

— *Suggested Mini-Lessons* —

◉ Provide each student with either the target idiom/slang words OR the translations. For instance, if a student has three idioms/slang words, another student has the matching three translations. Then, have students physically find the student who has their matches.

☑ Once students find each other, they work with the idioms/slang words that they just matched from pages 157-160.

☑ Each pair reads their section of assigned idioms and creates a sentence for the "**Now you do it**" section of the idioms. After completing, each pair shares their sample sentence with another pair.

◉ In pairs, students complete the **"Now you do it"** sections orally for each idiom. Each student in the pair must come up with a new sentence for each idiom.

LET'S PRACTICE!

TEXT PAGE 161-163:

◉ Students complete the practice activities on these pages independently first and then check their answers in pairs. After the pair check is complete, the answers are reviewed as a class.

⮕ *Challenge: Have students create their own "Find-The-Word Grids." Once they finish, they give their grid to a partner to solve.*

TEXT PAGES 164:

◉ Have students complete the matching activity independently before checking their answers with a partner and then reviewing as a class.

⮕ *Challenge: Provide each student with the target idiom/slang word from* **LET'S REVIEW** *on page 164 and have them draw a picture that represents that idiom. The student gives their picture to a partner, and the partner matches the definition from column C to the picture.*

WORKBOOK EXERCISES + EXPANSION

TEXT PAGES 165-169:

◉ Students can engage in the following expansion activities for both **THE SLANGMAN FILES** as well as the target idioms/slang presented in the unit:

1. **Written Production:** Have students create a dialogue or story with the target idioms/slang and perform it or read it in front of the class. Make it a contest! See which group can use the most idioms correctly in their dialogue/story.

2. **Spoken Production:** Have students engage in a timed role play in pairs in front of the class. Provide them each with a different set of target idioms/slang that they need to use during the role play.

3. **Visual Activity:** Have students play Pictionary® in groups. Each student chooses a target idiom/slang word from the unit and draws an image that captures the meaning. Group members will try to guess the correct idiom/slang word. The student who guesses the most idioms correctly in the group is the winner.

⮕ *Challenge: Students cannot use the textbook when they are guessing the idioms/slang words.*

POST-UNIT ACTIVITY:

⊙ As a class, tune in to **SLANGMAN FRIDAYS** which features a new episode on idioms and slang used on TV each week - **https://www.youtube.com/SlangmanTV** and *MAKE SURE THAT EACH STUDENT SUBSCRIBES!*

☑ The video can be used as a final component of the unit and used as a warm-up/review before the next unit begins. Optional activities for the warm-up/review include:

1. Fill in the blank activity with target slang/idioms used in the video.

2. Sentence creation with target idioms/slang.

3. Dialog/story creation with target idioms/slang.

4. *Teaching by students:* Assign each student or pair one of the idioms/slang words explained in the video and ask them to teach it to the rest of the class with at least one context example.

TEACHER NOTES

TEACHER'S GUIDE

LESSON PREP!

- ⊙ *Optional:* Prepare the target slang words/idioms in a song or story so that students can listen to the vocabulary in context. Provide a transcript for students to read while they listen.

- ⊙ Throughout the lesson, you'll see the following icons:  and

  ⮕ *This is a great opportunity to have your students take out their mobile devices and use the QR code to access the many audio and video programs that pertain to the lesson.*

LET'S WARM UP!

MATCH THE PICTURES

1. Students discuss the topic, **TO YOUR HEALTH**, in partners. The teacher can provide students with a handout of discussion questions.

Example questions:

☑ When was the last time you were sick?

☑ What is your least favorite part about going to the doctor?

☑ Have you ever had to go to the hospital? What happened?

☑ Would you ever want to be a doctor? Why or why not?

☑ Why do you think doctors get paid so much money?

2. The images represent the definition of the idioms/slang words both literally and figuratively. In partners, students discuss the images on pages 171 and 172 of the textbook. Have them describe what's happening in each photo.

PAGES 171-172:

◉ Students complete the matching activity on page 172 independently.

☑ Students check their answers in partners before reviewing as a class.

LET'S TALK!

TEXT PAGES 173-174:

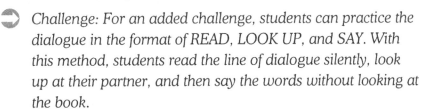

◉ Students take turns practicing the dialogues as Karen and Janet.

⟳ *Challenge: For an added challenge, students can practice the dialogue in the format of READ, LOOK UP, and SAY. With this method, students read the line of dialogue silently, look up at their partner, and then say the words without looking at the book.*

LET'S USE "REAL SPEAK!"

TEXT PAGES 175-176:

◉ Teacher presents the "Real Speak" rules to the class.

☑ Students practice the conversation on page 175 in partners using the "Real Speak" rule.

➲ *Challenge: READ, LOOK UP, and SAY. Again, students read the line of dialogue silently, look up at their partner, and then say the words without looking at the book.*

◉ In partners, students complete activity **D (UNSCRAMBLE)** on page 176 independently first and then check their answers in partners.

➲ *Challenge: Provide students with a set of complete sentences/questions from activity D on page 176. Have the student scramble the words for his/her partner. The partner should unscramble the sentence/question and then practice the target "Real Speak."*

LET'S LEARN!

TEXT PAGES 177-180:

— Suggested Mini-Lessons —

◉ Provide each student with an idiom/slang word from pages 177-180. Have each student draw a picture that represents his/her word or phrase.

☑ Have students get in small groups and try to guess the slang word/idiom associated with the pictures.

◉ Assign each student a section of idioms/slang words from pages 177-180.

☑ Each pair reads his/her section of assigned idioms and creates a sentence for the **"Now you do it"** section of the idioms. After completing, each pair shares their sample sentence with another pair.

◉ In pairs, students complete the **"Now you do it"** sections orally for each idiom. Each student in the pair must come up with a new sentence for each idiom.

LET'S PRACTICE!

TEXT PAGE 181-183:

◉ Students complete the practice activities on these pages independently fi̶̶̶ ̶̶̶ ̶̶̶check their answers in pairs. After the pair check is complete, the answers are reviewed as a class.

⮕ *Challenge: Have students, in partners, create their own completed conversation like the one on page 181 with target idioms provided to them. Have students perform their conversations in front of the class.*

TEXT PAGES 184:

◉ Have students complete the matching activity independently before checking their answers with a partner and then reviewing as a class.

⮕ *Challenge: Provide each pair of students with flash cards of column A, B, and C on page 184. Have students take turns turning over two flash cards to make matches until the pairs achieve all of the matches from the three columns.*

WORKBOOK EXERCISES + EXPANSION

TEXT PAGES 185–191:

◉ Students can engage in the following expansion activities for both **THE SLANGMAN FILES** as well as the target idioms/slang presented in the unit:

1. **Written Production:** Have students create a dialogue or story with the target idioms/slang and perform it or read it in front of the class. Make it a contest! See which group can use the most idioms correctly in their dialogue/story.

2. **Spoken Production:** Have students engage in a timed role play in pairs in front of the class. Provide them each with a different set of target idioms/slang that they need to use during the role play.

3. **Visual Activity:** Have students play Pictionary® in groups. Each student chooses a target idiom/slang word from the unit and draws an image that captures the meaning. Group members will try to guess the correct idiom/slang word. The student who guesses the most idioms correctly in the group is the winner.

⮕ *Challenge: Students cannot use the textbook when they are guessing the idioms/slang words.*

POST-UNIT ACTIVITY:

⊙ As a class, tune in to **SLANGMAN FRIDAYS** which features a new episode on idioms and slang used on TV each week - **https://www.youtube.com/SlangmanTV** and *MAKE SURE THAT EACH STUDENT SUBSCRIBES!*

☑ The video can be used as a final component of the unit and used as a warm-up/review before the next unit begins. Optional activities for the warm-up/review include:

1. Fill in the blank activity with target slang/idioms used in the video.

2. Sentence creation with target idioms/slang.

3. Dialog/story creation with target idioms/slang.

4. *Teaching by students:* Assign each student or pair one of the idioms/slang words explained in the video and ask them to teach it to the rest of the class with at least one context example.

TEACHER NOTES

TEACHER'S GUIDE

LESSON PREP!

- ⊙ *Optional*: Prepare the target slang words/idioms in a song or story so that students can listen to the vocabulary in context. Provide a transcript for students to read while they listen.

- ⊙ Throughout the lesson, you'll see the following icons:  and

  ➲ *This is a great opportunity to have your students take out their mobile devices and use the QR code to access the many audio and video programs that pertain to the lesson.*

LET'S WARM UP!

MATCH THE PICTURES

1. Students discuss the topic, **ON A DATE**, in partners. The teacher can provide students with a handout of discussion questions.

<u>Example questions:</u>

☑ What is the best date you've ever been on?

☑ What is the worst date you've ever been on?

☑ What is your favorite thing to do on a date?

☑ Do you get nervous for dates? What do you do to stay calm?

☑ Who do you think should pay on a date? Why?

2. The images represent the definition of the idioms/slang words both literally and figuratively. In partners, students discuss the images on pages 193 and 194 of the textbook. Have them describe what's happening in each photo.

PAGES 193-194:

◉ Students complete the matching activity on page 194 independently.

☑ Students check their answers in partners before reviewing as a class.

LET'S TALK!

TEXT PAGES 195-196:

◉ Students take turns practicing the dialogues as Melanie and Susan.

➲ *Challenge: For an added challenge, students can practice the dialogue in the format of READ, LOOK UP, and SAY. With this method, students read the line of dialogue silently, look up at their partner, and then say the words without looking at the book.*

LET'S USE "REAL SPEAK!"

TEXT PAGES 197-198:

◉ Teacher presents the "Real Speak" rules to the class.

☑ Students practice the conversation on page 197 in partners using the "Real Speak" rule.

➔ *Challenge: READ, LOOK UP, and SAY. Again, students read the line of dialogue silently, look up at their partner, and then say the words without looking at the book.*

◉ In partners, students complete activity **A (NOW YOU HAFTA DO A "HAFTA" EXERCISE)** on page 198 independently first and then check their answers in partners.

➔ *Challenge: Have students write their own recipes like the one on page 198. They can write about a recipe from their home culture. The student should leave the target "Real Speak" blank and have a partner try to fill them in. After, each student should practice their partner's recipe aloud, focusing on saying the "Real Speak" correctly.*

LET'S LEARN!

TEXT PAGES 199-202:

— *Suggested Mini-Lesson* —

◉ Provide students with the translations of the idioms/slang words in a word bank.

☑ Have students listen to the "Real Speak" versions of the idioms/slang words without looking in their textbooks.

☑ Have students write down the translation for each "Real Speak" version of the idiom/slang word.

◉ Assign each student a section of idioms/slang words from pages 199-202.

☑ Each student reads his/her section of assigned idioms and creates a sentence for the **"Now you do it"** section of the idioms. After completing, each student shares his/her sample sentence with a small group of.

◉ In pairs, students complete the **"Now you do it"** sections for each idiom. Each student in the pair must come up with a new sentence for each idiom.

LET'S PRACTICE!

TEXT PAGE 203-205:

⊙ Students complete the practice activities on these pages independently first and then check their answers in pairs. After the pair check is complete, the answers are reviewed as a class.

↪ *Challenge: Have students, in partners, write their own Cupid Gazette letters like the one on page 204. They should also leave blanks that correlate with page 203. The partners then trade their letters and fill in the blanks with their answers on page 203. Each pair takes turn reading their completed letter to the other pair.*

TEXT PAGES 206:

⊙ Have students complete the matching activity independently before checking their answers with a partner and then reviewing as a class.

↪ *Challenge: Provide each student with either a card from column A or column B. Have the students walk around and find their opposite. Once the students are matched, have them write a sentence using both of their target idioms/slang words. Then, they can share it with the class.*

WORKBOOK EXERCISES + EXPANSION

TEXT PAGES 207-211:

⊙ Students can engage in the following expansion activities for both **THE SLANGMAN FILES** as well as the target idioms/slang presented in the unit:

1. **Written Production:** Have students create a dialogue or story with the target idioms/slang and perform it or read it in front of the class. Make it a contest! See which group can use the most idioms correctly in their dialogue/story.

2. **Spoken Production:** Have students engage in a timed role play in pairs in front of the class. Provide them each with a different set of target idioms/slang that they need to use during the role play.

3. **Visual Activity:** Have students play Pictionary® in groups. Each student chooses a target idiom/slang word from the unit and draws an image that captures the meaning. Group members will try to guess the correct idiom/slang word. The student who guesses the most idioms correctly in the group is the winner.

➲ *Challenge: Students cannot use the textbook when they are guessing the idioms/slang words.*

POST-UNIT ACTIVITY:

◉ As a class, tune in to **SLANGMAN FRIDAYS** which features a new episode on idioms and slang used on TV each week - **https://www.youtube.com/SlangmanTV** and *MAKE SURE THAT EACH STUDENT SUBSCRIBES!*

☑ The video can be used as a final component of the unit and used as a warm-up/review before the next unit begins. Optional activities for the warm-up/review include:

1. Fill in the blank activity with target slang/idioms used in the video.

2. Sentence creation with target idioms/slang.

3. Dialog/story creation with target idioms/slang.

4. *Teaching by students:* Assign each student or pair one of the idioms/slang words explained in the video and ask them to teach it to the rest of the class with at least one context example.

TEACHER NOTES

Made in the
USA
Columbia, SC